Abu Bakr as-Siddiq

Translated by
Sara Saleem

Ta-Ha Publishers Ltd.
1, Wynne Road
London SW9 0BB

Reprinted 1999

Published by

Ta-Ha Publishers Ltd.
1 Wynne Road
London SW9 0BB
website:http://www.taha.co.uk/
email: sales@taha.co.uk

Translated by: Sara Saleem
General Editor: Afsar Siddiqui
Edited by: Abdassamad Clarke
Illustrated by: M. Ishaq

A catalogue record for this book is available from the British Library

ISBN 1 897940 47 5

Typeset by: Abdassamad Clarke.

Printed and Bound by- De-Luxe Printers,
London NW10 7NR.

Contents

بسم الله الرحمن الرحيم

The First Public Speaker

Muhammad ibn Abdullah صلى الله عليه وسلم of the tribe of Quraysh, was made a prophet by Allah to proclaim the message of his Creator and Sustainer.

The Prophet صلى الله عليه وسلم began to tell close friends and family about the Oneness of Allah, to call them to worship Allah and keep away from bad things. Abu Bakr رضي الله عنه became the first adult man to accept Islam from the Prophet Muhammad صلى الله عليه وسلم just as the Prophet's wife Khadijah رضي الله عنها was the first woman.

Abu Bakr passionately wanted to spread the word of Allah. He decided to take the message to the chiefs of Quraysh. First, he told the Prophet صلى الله عليه وسلم what he meant to do.

At first the Noble Prophet صلى الله عليه وسلم did not agree to let him go, but Abu Bakr asked him urgently. Then Allah gave him the revelation which told him to proclaim Islam openly. So the Messenger of Allah صلى الله عليه وسلم gave him permission.

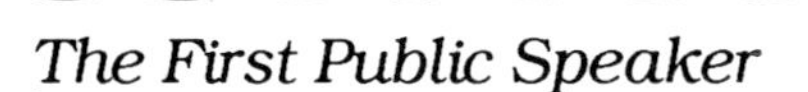

Abu Bakr stood up and addressed the chiefs of Quraysh as they sat around the Ka'bah. He called them to believe in Allah, and to worship Him alone. The Messenger of Allah ﷺ sat and listened to his speech. It was the very first time men were invited to Allah and His Prophet.

Unfortunately, Abu Bakr's words did not have the desired effect on Quraysh. Soon after he stood up to talk, they beat him and the other Muslims violently.

The struggle continued until some people from Abu Bakr's clan, Bani Tamim, approached. The attackers scattered. Abu Bakr was carried to his house. People thought that he would not survive his injuries.

Four men wrapped Abu Bakr in some cloth and laid him out on a bed in his house. Then they returned to the Ka'bah, pledging, if Abu Bakr died, to kill the man who had attacked him.

Meanwhile at the house, Abu Bakr's mother, Umm al-Khair Salma, watched anxiously over him. Abu Bakr remained in a deep slumber. As the sun was about to set, Abu Bakr made a slight movement. He opened his eyes and asked, "How is the Messenger of Allah?"

His mother was relieved to hear him speak and asked him, "How are you feeling, Abu Bakr?"

He merely asked again, "How is the Messenger

of Allah?"

"I do not know," she replied.

"Go to Fatimah bint al-Khattab and ask her about him," he said. Fatimah was a Muslim and she was the sister of Umar ibn al-Khattab who was not yet a Muslim.

She got up immediately and went to Fatimah's house. She told Fatimah that Abu Bakr was asking about the safety of Muhammad ibn Abd-ullah.

"I do not know how he is," Fatimah replied, trying to keep her Islam secret, "But if you want I'll go with you to see Abu Bakr."

Both women went and sat beside Abu Bakr.

"How is the Messenger of Allah?" he asked Fatimah.

"Your mother is listening," she said. She was nervous because Salma was not a Muslim.

"Don't worry," said Abu Bakr.

"The Messenger of Allah is safe and well. He is at the house of Ibn al-Arqam," she said.

Salma took a bowl of milk to her son and said, "Take this and drink my son. It will make you stronger."

Abu Bakr replied, "No, by Allah, I won't eat or drink anything until I have seen the Messenger of Allah."

They waited until night had fallen. Then, they

took Abu Bakr, Salma supporting his right arm and Fatimah his left arm. Slowly the three of them made their way to the house of al-Arqam. Abu Bakr went straight away to the room where the Prophet ﷺ.

The Messenger of Allah ﷺ rose to his feet and greeted him. He asked, "How are you Abu Bakr?"

"Messenger of Allah, you who are dearer to me than my own father and mother, nothing happened to me except what that godless person did to my face," Abu Bakr told him.

The Prophet ﷺ prayed for his wellbeing.

Abu Bakr رضي الله عنه said, "This is my mother, who is devoted to her son. Please invite her to Islam. Allah has been kind to her, and maybe He will save her from the Fire if you invite her to accept Islam."

So the Prophet ﷺ invited her to put her trust in Allah, exalted is He. Within a few minutes Salma repeated the *shahadah,* "I witness that there is no god but Allah and that Muhammad is the Messenger of Allah." His mother's embracing Islam must have pleased Abu Bakr.

With this event, Abu Bakr who was the first adult man to accept Islam became the first to publicly call people to Islam and one of the first Muslims to suffer for the sake of Allah the Exalted.

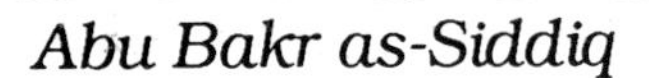

* * *

Even before accepting Islam, Abu Bakr was well-known in Makkah. He kept away from the bad behaviour of the Arabs of his time. Most importantly he did not worship the idols of stone his fellow Arabs worshipped. He explained why, "When I was about fourteen, my father, Abu Qahafah, took me by the hand and led me to a room in which there were some stone idols. He told me, 'Here are your gods,' and he left me there and went away. I approached the stone idols and said, 'I'm hungry. Feed me!' But I received no answer, so I threw stones at them."

Abu Bakr used this intelligence well, after he became a Muslim to convince old friends to accept Islam. These men themselves were very capable people. They in turn spread the message of Islam.

When he became a Muslim he was a prosperous merchant. His wealth amounted to around fourteen thousand of the silver coins called Dirhams. After his Islam he spent most of that on needy people and in the Way of Allah. He bought Muslim slaves from their oppressive idol-worshipping owners. When he had paid for them, he would set them free for the sake of Allah. He set free Zinnirah ar-Rumiyyah.

It is said that when Zinnirah was freed she had

gone completely blind. Quraysh said that it was their idols al-Laat and al-Uzza who had taken her sight away. Zinnirah, who had become a Muslim, would say, "By Allah this is not the case. Al-Laat and al-Uzza can't harm or heal." Allah gave her back her sight,

So Abu Bakr spent his wealth on freeing slaves and on the poor people of the city. The spending of wealth in the way of Allah is praised in many *ayat* of the Noble Qur'an:

> **"Those who believe and emigrate and strive in the way of Allah with their wealth and with their selves, they have the highest place in the view of Allah; and they are the victorious."**
> **(Qur'an, Surah al-Anfal: 72)**

The First Companion

Abu Bakr رضي الله عنه remained a close companion of the Prophet Muhammad صلى الله عليه وسلم after his Islam. Quraysh inflicted very heavy suffering on the Muslims. Then the Prophet صلى الله عليه وسلم gave many of the Companions permission to emigrate to Abyssinia.

Abu Bakr asked the Messenger of Allah صلى الله عليه وسلم to be allowed to emigrate with the other Muslims. The Prophet said yes and Abu Bakr left Makkah. A few days later, he arrived at a place called Burk al-Ghimad, not far from the Red Sea. Here he met an Arab chief called Ibn ad-Dughanna. He had known Abu Bakr in his days of wealth and influence. He was surprised to see him there in such a state.

He asked Abu Bakr, "Where are you going?"

"My tribe has made me leave," he said, "Now I just want to travel the earth so that I can worship my Creator."

Ibn ad-Dughanna exclaimed, "Why, by Allah,

you are the ornament of your tribe, you help the poor, you do good and earn nothing from this for yourself! Someone like you, Abu Bakr, cannot leave. Come back with me under my protection and worship your Creator in your own land."

Abu Bakr agreed, and went back with Ibn ad-Dughanna. When they reached Makkah, Ibn ad-Dughanna went to the Ka'bah and announced to the tribal chiefs seated in its courtyard, "Quraysh, I have engaged the services of Abu Bakr. Do not approach him unless it is with good intentions."

Abu Bakr ﵁ had a place for prayer near the gate of his house. He was a very softhearted man. Whenever he would recite the beautiful *ayat* of Qur'an, his eyes would overflow with tears. The children, women and servants of the area where he lived would stop outside the gate and marvel at the way he prayed.

The elders of Quraysh became quite perturbed at the effect this had on them. They went to Ibn ad-Dughanna and told him, "Ibn ad-Dughanna, surely you didn't hire this man to injure us? When he prays and recites, he becomes more emotional than Muhammad himself, who has a way of conducting himself. We are afraid that our children and women and the weak among us, they might be tempted to follow him. Tell him to

go into his house and do whatever he wants inside it."

Ibn ad-Dughanna went and said to Abu Bakr, "Abu Bakr, I did not engage your services to offend anyone. They do not like you praying in the place where you now do. Go into your house and do whatever you like inside it."

Abu Bakr saw that his seeking refuge with Ibn ad-Dughanna or with any other non-Muslim was not fitting. The protection of Allah is greater and everlasting. Abu Bakr said, "I give you back your protection and am pleased to have the protection of Allah."

Ibn ad-Dughanna made sure that Abu Bakr had made up his mind. Then he went to the Ka'bah and shouted, "Quraysh! The son of Abu Qahafah has renounced my protection, so you are now responsible for your own actions."

Just then, Abu Bakr came walking up to the Ka'bah. Some of the fools of Quraysh met him. They threw dust on his head. Al-As ibn Wa'il, from Abu Bakr's tribe, happened to be passing.

Abu Bakr called out to him, "Can't you see what these idiots are doing?"

Al-As just replied, "It's your own fault."

Abu Bakr رضي الله عنه then repeated, as if to himself, "O Allah, there is none more gentle than You, O Allah there is none more gentle than You..."

* * *

The Messenger of Allah صلى الله عليه وسلم and Khadijah رضي الله عنها had been happily married for twenty-five years. She had given birth to four daughters who lived to grow up, and two sons who died young. It was about ten years after the Messenger of Allah صلى الله عليه وسلم first received the revelation that Khadijah died.

At this difficult time, the Prophet Muhammad صلى الله عليه وسلم made his miraculous *Isra'* – Night Journey to the Furthest Mosque in Jerusalem. From there he went on the *Mi'raj* – the ascent into the heavens. This unique event took place during one night. When he returned, he went to the Ka'bah. He told the people there of his visit to Jerusalem, and his meeting with the Prophets عليهم السلام.

A group of the *kuffar* accused the Prophet صلى الله عليه وسلم of madness. They went to Abu Bakr's house and asked, "What do you think of your friend now?" They told him what the Messenger of Allah صلى الله عليه وسلم had said.

Abu Bakr calmly said, "If that is what he says, then it is true. What is astonishing about that? He tells me that tidings come to him from heaven in an hour of the day or the night, and I know that he is speaking the truth. That is even more astonishing than the news that you bring."

Abu Bakr went to the Ka'bah and repeated his affirmation of the Prophet's journey. It was for this great trust that the Prophet ﷺ gave him the title *As-Siddiq* – 'The Confirmer of the Truth'.

* * *

The Prophet ﷺ would often visit Abu Bakr and his wife Umm Ruman. It was about a year after the death of Khadijah that the Prophet ﷺ saw in a dream that he would one day marry A'ishah, Abu Bakr's daughter. He did not mention the dream to anyone, not even Abu Bakr, because A'ishah was still a young girl and promised in marriage to someone else. The Messenger of Allah ﷺ would say, "If this is from Allah, He will bring it to pass." Indeed Allah did make it happen, and the two families were brought much closer by the relationship.

* * *

Islam spread amongst the people of Makkah. Later it also spread among the people of Yathrib, the city later to be known as Madinah. The people of Madinah made an agreement with the Messenger of Allah ﷺ to spend of their wealth and their selves and to strive in the way of Allah. The Messenger of Allah ﷺ saw that many of his companions were suffering in Makkah. He allowed them to emigrate to Madinah. He himself stayed waiting for the command of Allah.

Abu Bakr asked the Prophet Muhammad ﷺ if he should go to Madinah. The Prophet ﷺ advised him, "Do not be hasty, perhaps Allah will give you a companion (for the journey)." By 'companion', the Prophet ﷺ meant himself. Abu Bakr was pleased with this answer. Nearly all of the Companions left Makkah, except for Ali رضي الله عنه and Abu Bakr رضي الله عنه.

When Abu Bakr رضي الله عنه was told that he would soon accompany the Prophet ﷺ to Madinah, he prepared for the trip. He bought two camels and fed them every day, so that they would be ready for the journey.

One day soon after that, the command came to the Prophet ﷺ to emigrate. That was on the same day that Quraysh made up their minds to kill him. The angel Jibril عليه السلام came with the command to the Prophet. He went immediately to the house of Abu Bakr and told him that they must now emigrate. Abu Bakr رضي الله عنه wept for joy.

Jibril عليه السلام had warned the Prophet ﷺ that Quraysh were plotting to kill him. The Messenger of Allah ﷺ told Ali ibn Abi Talib of the plot. Ali رضي الله عنه stayed behind to return all the goods which Quraysh had entrusted to the Prophet ﷺ.

While Ali slept in the Messenger's bed, the Messenger ﷺ and Abu Bakr رضي الله عنه set off to Madinah. In the morning Quraysh discovered their plan had been foiled. They offered one hundred camels to whoever found the Prophet ﷺ.

Madinah is northwest of Makkah. They headed south in order to trick Quraysh and took refuge in Mount Thawr. Abdullah, Abu Bakr's son, concealed the camels while they hid in the cave for some days. Asma, his other daughter, brought them food every day. One evening while they were in the cave, they heard the voices of five or six men from Quraysh outside. Abu Bakr was anxious that the Prophet ﷺ was in danger. But the Prophet ﷺ calmly reassured him saying, "Why do you fear for two of whom Allah is the third? Do not be sad for Allah is with us."

They heard footsteps coming nearer to the cave. They heard men's voices outside saying that there really was no need to look inside as there could not be anyone there. When the Messenger and Abu Bakr went to the mouth of the cave after the men had gone, they found that a spider had spun a web from an acacia tree, just outside, to the wall of the cave. Also just inside the cave, a bird had made its nest and was perched in it. It looked as if no-one had gone into the cave for a very long time.

After they reached Madinah, the Messenger of Allah made brotherhood between the *Muhajirun* – the people who had emigrated from Makkah – and some of the *Ansar*– the Muslims of Madinah. Each Madinan man shared everything with his brother from Makkah. Abu Bakr became the brother of Kharijah ibn Zaid.

The Prophet ﷺ made a treaty with the Jews allowing them freedom to practise their own worship of God. The Companions still knew the importance of telling them about Islam. One day, Abu Bakr رضي الله عنه went to a gathering of the Jews and met a rabbi called Finhas. Abu Bakr said to him, "Surely you know that Muhammad is the Messenger of Allah. He brought you the Truth...you will find that you also possess it, written in the *Tawrah* and in the *Injil*."

The rabbi arrogantly replied, "By Allah, Abu Bakr, we have no need of Allah. Rather He has need of us. We will not humiliate ourselves before Him as He has humiliated Himself before us... If He did not need us then why should He ask us to give Him a loan as your Companion (the Prophet ﷺ) claims, forbidding you from giving and taking interest while allowing us interest?"

The rabbi quoted to Abu Bakr the words from the Noble Qur'an:

"Whoever lends Allah a beautiful loan, it will be multiplied for him many times."

Abu Bakr was furious at the rabbi's words. He hit the rabbi in the face and said, "By Allah, who has my life in His hands, if it were not for the treaty which we have, I would have given your

head a good beating, enemy of Allah!"

Finhas went straight to the Prophet ﷺ and complained about the slap Abu Bakr had given him.

The Prophet ﷺ asked Abu Bakr. "What made you do it?"

"Messenger of Allah," replied Abu Bakr رضي الله عنه, "This enemy of Allah ... claimed that Allah needs him and that he himself does not need Allah. When he said this, I became angry for the sake of Allah and hit his face."

The rabbi denied what Abu Bakr said, but Allah sent down these *ayat* of the Qur'an confirming him:

"Allah has heard the words of those who say, 'Allah is needy and we are free from all want'. We will record what they say and their killing of the prophets without any right. We say, 'Taste the punishment of the Fire. That is what your hands have sent forward'. Truly, Allah does not oppress the slaves (of Allah)." (Qur'an, Surah Ali 'Imran: 181)

* * *

In the second year after the Hijrah (the Emigration), the Battle of Badr took place. It is the first battle in Islam. On the day of Badr, the Messenger of Allah ﷺ prayed, "O Allah, give me what

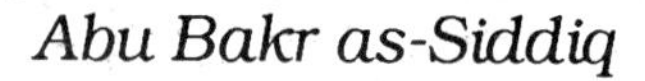

You have promised me. O Allah, if this small band of Muslims is defeated, there will be no-one left on the earth to worship You."

He kept asking his Lord. Abu Bakr said, "Prophet of Allah, your constant asking will annoy your Lord. Allah will fulfil His promise to you."

When the battle was about to begin, Sa'd ibn Mu'adh said, "Prophet of Allah, why don't we build a shelter for you, and place your camels in readiness beside it? Then we will go to meet our enemy. If Allah blesses us with victory over our enemy, then that is what we desire. If not you can mount your camel and catch up with those of us who have been left behind."

The Prophet ﷺ agreed with Sa'd and a shelter was built. The Companions agreed that Abu Bakr and others should stay and protect the Prophet ﷺ. Much of the time the Prophet ﷺ was out exhorting his men to fight.

Abu Bakr رضي الله عنه fought so bravely that day, that Ali ibn Abi Talib رضي الله عنه, himself the bravest of warriors, said, "Abu Bakr is the bravest of men."

* * *

Then later, the Muslims conquered Makkah, with almost no fighting. Abu Bakr brought his aged father to meet the Prophet. When the Prophet ﷺ saw him, he said to Abu Bakr, "Why did you not leave your father in his house until I was

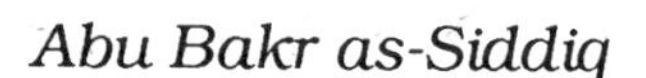

able to come and visit him?"

Abu Bakr replied, "Messenger of Allah, it is more proper that he should walk to see you than that you should walk to see him."

Then the Prophet ﷺ turned to Abu Qahafah, and returned his greeting with a better one.

* * *

Nine years after the Hijrah, the Messenger ﷺ sent Abu Bakr to lead the Hajj. The next year, the Messenger himself ﷺ led the Hajj, the Farewell Pilgrimage. Some time afterwards, the Prophet of Allah ﷺ felt his last illness beginning. One day he went out of his house, his head wrapped in a turban. He looked towards the doors of some of the Companions' houses which opened into the mosque. The walls of their houses were also the walls of the mosque. The Prophet ﷺ said, "See to these doors that open on to the mosque and shut them except the one from Abu Bakr's house, for I know no one who is a better friend to me than him."

After the Prophet ﷺ returned to his house, his illness increased. At the time of prayer, he called Bilal and said, "Tell Abu Bakr to lead the people in prayer."

Bilal (رضي الله عنه) went, but could not find Abu Bakr, so he told Umar ibn al-Khattab to lead the people in prayer. When the Messenger of Allah ﷺ heard

Umar's voice saying "Allahu Akbar", he said, "Where is Abu Bakr? Allah and the Muslims refuse this. Allah and the Muslims refuse this." Then he called for Abu Bakr again and he was found and led the prayers.

After that, the health of the Messenger of Allah improved slightly. Abu Bakr went to see him and said, "Messenger of Allah, I see that by the grace of Allah you have become as we like to see you."

Then he asked if could go to visit a house where one of his wives lived and he was given permission. While he was there he received the news of the passing of the Messenger of Allah صلى الله عليه وسلم. He hurried to A'ishah's house. The Prophet was laid out in a corner of the room covered with a cloth. Abu Bakr leant towards him and lifted the cloth from his face and kissed it farewell. He said, "You are (dearer to me than) my father and mother. As for the death which has been decreed for you by Allah, you have now tasted it. After this, you will never again be afflicted with death."

He put the cover back on his face and left the room. Then he saw the Muslims gathered outside the mosque listening to Umar, who was saying, "People, the Messenger of Allah has not died, but has gone to his Lord in the same way as Musa ibn Imran went."

Abu Bakr signalled to him and told him to be

quiet, then he said, "People, whoever worshipped Muhammad then Muhammad is dead. Whoever worships Allah, then Allah is the Living who does not die."

Then he recited the words of Allah, the Exalted: **"Muhammad is but a prophet, and prophets have passed away before him. If he dies or is killed, will you then turn on your heels? Whoever turns on his heels, then, will do no harm to Allah. Allah will reward those who are thankful." (Qur'an, Surah Ali 'Imran: 144)**

When they heard this *ayah*, it was as if it had only been revealed on that day.

The First Successor

A man came rushing towards Abu Bakr and Umar while they stood watching the people disperse and said, "The Ansar have gathered in the dwellings of the Bani Sa'idah.

Abu Bakr said to Umar, "Let us go to our brothers the Ansar and see what is happening."

When they arrived they found a discussion was going on as to whether the successor to the Prophet ﷺ should be from the Ansar or the Muhajirun. Abu Bakr stood and beckoned them to listen to him. He said, "We are the Muhajirun and you are the Ansar, our brothers in faith, our partners in sharing the spoils of war, and our helpers against the enemy. Whatever good you have mentioned about yourselves is true. You are indeed of all the people of this earth, most worthy of praise ... but from amongst us are the leaders and from amongst you the deputies."

After saying this, Abu Bakr took the hand of Umar ibn al-Khattab and the hand of Abu Ubaidah ibn al-Jarrah, and said, “Which one of these two men will you be content with (as Khalifah)?”

Umar said, “No, by Allah! We will not take this command away from you, for you are the best of the Muhajirun, and you were the second person in the cave (with the Prophet). You were the successor of the Prophet ﷺ in leading the prayers; and prayer is the best of the Muslims' faith. Who else should we entrust this office to but you? Give us your hand so that we may pledge allegiance to you.”

Umar and Abu Ubaidah pledged allegiance, after which everyone else followed, recognising Abu Bakr as the first Khalifah or Successor of the Messenger of Allah ﷺ.

After they had sworn allegiance to Abu Bakr, he went to the place where the body of the Messenger of Allah ﷺ was being prepared for burial. Ali, Shaqran and Usamah ibn Zaid were washing the body. They wrapped it in three pieces of Yemeni cloth and placed it on a bed. The Muslims then came to perform the funeral prayer, group after group. Then the women and children came.

The first of the men to enter were Abu Bakr and Umar and a group of the Muhajirun and Ansar, as many as the house would allow. When the time for burial came, the people disagreed as to where he should be buried. Abu Bakr رضي الله عنه

settled the question by repeating what he had heard the Prophet ﷺ say, "Whenever a prophet dies, he is always buried where he died." The Muslims buried the Messenger of Allah ﷺ in a grave dug beneath the floor of A'ishah's room where he had breathed his last.

When the Muslims had finished the burial, Abu Bakr stood and praised Allah, and gave his first *khutbah* as Khalifah of the Messenger of Allah. He said:

> "People, I have been given authority over you, though I am not the best of you. If I do good, then obey me, but if I do wrong, then put me right. Truth is a trust and dishonesty is treachery. The weak among you are strong until I have given them their rights, insha'Allah. None of you must give up *jihad,* for no nation has given up *jihad* but that Allah has punished it. Obey me if I follow Allah and His Messenger. If I disobey Allah and His Messenger, then I have no right to your obedience. Stand up for prayer, may Allah have mercy on you."

* * *

The next morning, Abu Bakr was on his way to the market. He met Abu Ubaidah and Umar. Umar asked him, "Where are you going, Khalifah of the Messenger of Allah?"

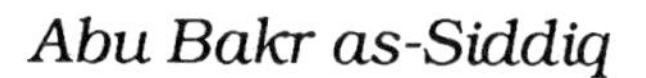

"I am going to the market," he replied.

"Why are you going there now that you have been entrusted with the leadership of the Muslims?" Umar asked.

"How am I going to feed my family?" Abu Bakr asked.

"Come with us so that we can allocate you something (as a salary)," they said.

All three of them set off. They allocated Abu Bakr the sum of two-hundred and fifty Dinars. However, Abu Bakr's previous income had been twice as much as this. To make ends meet he still had to go to the market to earn his living. When they realised this, they allocated him three hundred Dinars, and a sheep a day for his very large family. The Commander of the Believers was content with that.

* * *

The first issue which Abu Bakr faced as Khalifah was the army of Usamah ibn Zaid. Usamah, the leader of the army, was nineteen. The Companions did not agree to sending the army away at that moment and they did not agree to Usamah leading it.

But Abu Bakr remembered that the Prophet صلى الله عليه وسلم had said, "If you challenge his authority, you are challenging the authority of his father before him. By Allah, he was created for leadership. By

Allah, he is one of the people most loved by me after him (his father)."

Abu Bakr made up his mind to send the army of Usamah. When Umar went to see Abu Bakr, Abu Bakr said, "By He who has my life in His hands, even if I thought I would be attacked by a lion, I would still send Usamah, just as the Messenger of Allah ordered, even if I were the last person left to carry it out."

When Umar saw how determined Abu Bakr was to send the army, he asked that Abu Bakr send one of the military heroes of Islam, such as Khalid ibn al-Walid. Abu Bakr was adamant.

The army of Usamah came to play an important role. It put fear into the hearts of the Arabs who had renounced Islam after the death of the Prophet ﷺ. These tribes refused to pay the *zakah*. They thought that Islam itself would die after the Prophet had gone. They thought the Muslims had not the strength to raise an army. They did not imagine the Muslims would begin a new war against the Romans. Usamah left to fight the Romans. The Arabs were impressed.

In his fight against the tribes Abu Bakr sent out eleven armies. A lot of the Companions were killed, including many who had learnt the Qur'an by heart. But these battles saved Islam from being wiped out by the renegade Arabs.

The First Conqueror of Islam

The military commanders returned from their successful campaigns. Abu Bakr decided to send the armies North East and West to fight the two greatest military powers in the world at that time. These were the Byzantine Empire to the North and West and the Persian Empire in the North and East.

Muslim men came forward in huge numbers, from the Yemen, and from all corners of Arabia. Abu Bakr spoke to them:

"Do not give up the *jihad*, for there has been no nation that gave up *jihad* which has not been punished by Allah. In the Book of Allah a (special) reward is mentioned for struggling in the way of Allah. A Muslim must pay special attention to this. Allah has guided us to this as a means of saving ourselves from shame, and of honouring us in this world and the next. O people, the Messenger of Allah decided to turn his attention to Syria

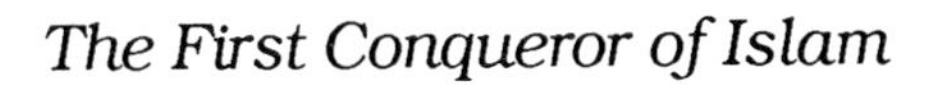

before he died. I have resolved to send Muslims to Syria with their property."

The armies went together to Syria and split there in four to cover four separate areas. Heraclius, the Byzantine emperor wanted to compromise and split Syria in half with the Muslims. The Muslims did not agree and they united again to fight him at Yarmuk. The fight was long and bitter but the Muslims eventually won.

At the same time another army was in Iraq preparing to fight the Persian empire. In Abu Bakr's brief time as Khalifah both Syria and Iraq began to come under the banner of Islam.

* * *

One day Umar went to the house of Abu Bakr and said to him, "I have brought you an important matter." He explained that many Qur'an reciters had been killed in recent battles and he was afraid that the Qur'an itself might disappear. He wanted the Khalifah to order that all the different *surahs* and *ayahs* of Qur'an which had been written down separately should be gathered together in one book.

Abu Bakr asked, "How can I do something that the Messenger of Allah ﷺ didn't do?" But Umar convinced him that it had to be done.

Abu Bakr ordered Zaid ibn Thabit, a young man of Madinah to do the job.

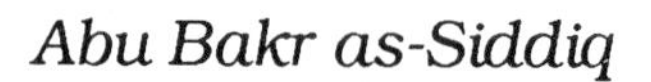

Zaid said, "By Allah, if you had told me to move a mountain, it would not have been heavier for me than telling me to gather together the Qur'an." Abu Bakr and Umar convinced him that it had to be done. So it is because of their work that today we have the written copies of Qur'an which are exactly the same as how people recited and wrote the Qur'an in Madinah. As Allah, the Exalted, says:

> **"Truly, We have sent down the Reminder (the Qur'an), and truly, We guard it."**
> **(Qur'an, Surah al-Hijr: 9)**

* * *

Abu Bakr was Khalifah of the Muslims for two and a half years. He saved Islam from Arab rebellions and established the government of Islam over a vast area. Then in 13 AH he fell ill. He knew that he was dying and that he must leave someone to rule the Muslims. After taking the advice of the Companions he knew that his own decision to appoint Umar was the right one. The Muslims count his placing Umar as Khalifah of the Muslims one of the greatest of his many good actions. It was in Umar's time that Islam expanded enormously.

Abu Bakr رضي الله عنه died and was buried next to the Prophet صلى الله عليه وسلم.